LISTEN!

Other resources
by Marilyn Shenenberger
and James Jordan
available from GIA Publications, Inc.

Evoking Sound: The Choral Warm-Up
Method, Procedures, Planning, and
Core Vocal Exercises (G-6397)
Accompanist Supplement with Accompaniment CD (G-6397A)
Compact Disc of Accompaniments (G-6397CD)

Ear Training Immersion Exercises for Choirs:
Choral Exercises in All the Modes (G-6429)
Ensemble Edition (spiral-bound) (G-6429A)
Choral Ensemble Intonation: Method, Procedure, and Exercises (G-5527T)
Choral Ensemble Intonation: Teaching Procedures Video (VHS-500)

Other resources
by James Jordan

The Musician's Walk: An Ethical Labyrinth (G-6734)
The Musician's Spirit (G-5866)
The Musican's Soul (G-5095)

Evoking Sound (G-4257) and Video/DVD with Heather Buchanan (VHS-530; DVD-530)

Choral Ensemble Intonation (Methods, Procedures, and Exercises) with Matthew Mehaffey (G-5527T)
and Teaching Procedures Video (VHS-500)
Intonation Exercises Octavo (G-5527I) and Modal Exercises Octavo (G-5527M)

Learn Conducting Technique with the Swiss Exercise Ball:
Developing Kinclusive Conducting Awareness
(G-6478)

Evoking Sound Choral Series
(James Jordan, editor)

LISTEN!

INTRODUCTORY HARMONIC IMMERSION SOLFEGE
FOR INDIVIDUALS AND CHOIRS

Student Edition

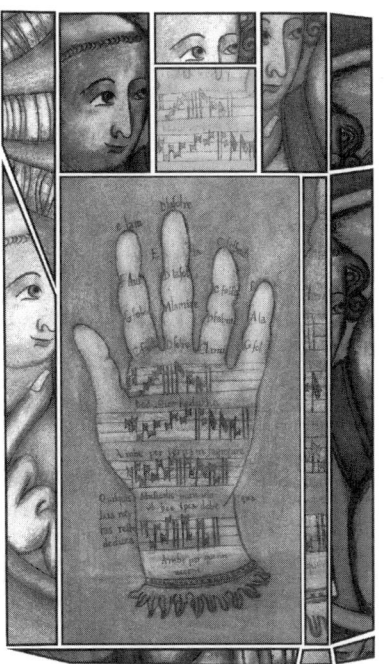

BOOK 1

MAJOR: TONIC, DOMINANT, AND SUBDOMINANT

MARILYN SHENENBERGER
WITH
JAMES JORDAN

GIA Publications, Inc.
Chicago

To my mother,
Anne Whitmire,
who started me on my musical journey.

My love of harmony is rooted in the
duets she sang with me when I was
a child and in her tireless devotion
and persistence in keeping me practicing.

Listen! Introductory Harmonic Immersion Solfege for Individuals and Choirs
Student Book One
Major: Tonic, Dominant, and Subdominant

Marilyn Shenenberger
with James Jordan

G-6971A
ISBN-13: 978-1-57999-614-7

Layout by Martha Chlipala

GIA Publications, Inc.
7404 South Mason Avenue, Chicago 60638
www.giamusic.com

Contents

UNIT IV – CHORD PROGRESSIONS WITH TONIC, DOMINANT, SUBDOMINANT

Four-Measure Progressions

Chord Progression Round

How to Use This Book

Directions for the exercises on the interactive CD are printed in your book. Many exercises are listening exercises only and, therefore, do not have scores.

This is an experiential lesson book! Each of the sections in this book is specifically designed to be used with the included interactive CD. It is imperative that the two be used together, in the order suggested, as each new exercise is dependent upon the previous exercise.

We learn to speak by listening to the language as it is spoken naturally by those around us. We absorb the patterns and syntax of the language by listening long before we are taught to associate the printed words with the sound of the words. Children are improvising with the words they have heard long before they can read them from a book and years before they are formally taught to construct a sentence using nouns, verbs, adverbs, etc.

After listening to absorb the sounds of the harmonic building blocks of simple major chord progressions, you will be encouraged to imitate as well as improvise using what you have absorbed. Only then will you be asked to link those sounds to the printed score.

The exercises, suitable for elementary through adult singers, are designed to familiarize you, the singer, with the primary major chords: tonic, dominant, and subdominant. It is important that these exercises be performed staccato, with space between each note. This will allow you to hear the next pitch internally before singing it. The chords are performed on the recording in a variety of inversions and broken chords by four singers from The Westminster Choir College. The four model voices on the recording are Katie Muka, soprano; Heather Kayan, alto; Reid Masters, tenor; and Mike O'Leary, bass. You will be guided through a sequence of listening, audiating, and imitating activities, first listening only to the model voice on the CD, then remembering what you heard in the following measures, and, last, imitating what you have heard.

After the groundwork has been laid through aural immersion, by listening and absorbing the sound of each of these chords, solfege syllables are added. The same exercises are then experienced a second time on this new level. Finally, after you know the sound of the chords and their names, you will be asked to follow along in the score. Music reading will occur as a by-product of the listening process.

I hope that through this total immersion into the three chords, which delineate the major cadence, you will notice improved listening skills, be more at ease improvising and creating your own patterns, and find it easier to relate what you hear to the printed page.

—Marilyn Shenenberger

UNIT I

TONIC CHORD INVERSIONS AND PATTERNS

Tonic Chord Solfege Syllable Pronunciation Guide

Actual Written Syllable	Correct Pronunciation
Do	**Doo** The tongue must lie flat in the mouth with the tip of the tongue resting lightly behind the font teeth. Imagine there is a pit in the tongue. The lips should look like "oo" and be rounded but without tension.
Mi	**Mee** Tongue position is high with the tip of the tongue anchored against the lower front teeth. The lips should be slightly rounded to promote focus in the vowel.
Sol	**Soo** This should be pronounced exactly as the "doo" above but beginning with "s."

Tonic Chord Inversions

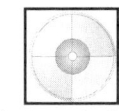

TRACKS 1–5

Exercise 1

LISTEN ONLY

A. TRACK 1: Listen to the different inversions of the tonic chord.

B. After you have absorbed the patterns, audiate them (hear them inside your head, without the sound being present).

C. TRACK 2: Audiate the inversions while listening to the accompaniment track.

Exercise 2

LISTEN AND SING

A. TRACK 3: The inversions will be sung one at a time on neutral syllables. Echo the pattern in the accompaniment measures following each inversion.

B. TRACK 4: Listen to the inversions sung on solfege syllables.

C. TRACK 5: The inversions will be sung one at a time on solfege syllables. Echo the pattern in the accompaniment measures following each inversion.

Tonic Chord Inversions

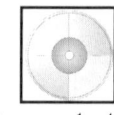

Exercise 3

LISTEN, SING, AND FOLLOW THE SCORE

A. TRACK 1: Follow the score for **Exercise 3** as you listen.

B. TRACK 1: Follow the score and sing along with Track 1 on neutral syllables. (Two different keys are used for these exercises so you can become familiar with reading the tonic chord on lines as well as spaces.)

C. TRACK 4: Follow the score and sing along with Track 4 on solfege syllables.

Tonic Inversions

Tracks 1, 4

5

Tonic Chord Patterns

Exercise 4

TRACK 6: Listen to the tonic chord patterns along with the aural accompaniment anchors, which sound the tonic and dominant. (There is no score for this exercise.)

Exercise 5

A. TRACK 7: Follow the score for **Exercise 5** to track the sound. Listen to each pattern sung individually. In the following measure, audiate the pattern you just heard (hear it without singing it). All the patterns will be sung first on a neutral syllable and repeated on solfege syllables when the exercise is reported.

B. TRACK 7: Listen to this track again, and in the measure following each pattern sing back the pattern you just heard sung for you.

Tonic Chord Patterns

Track 7

Exercise 6.

Tonic Chord Patterns

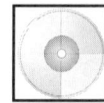

Exercise 6

  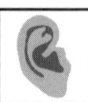

TRACK 8: Each pattern is repeated four times. In this exercise, *you sing the pattern first* on "doo," and the vocal model echoes you. Then, you sing the same pattern on solfege syllables, echoed again by the vocal model. This will allow you to check your accuracy and make any necessary corrections.

Tonic Chord Patterns

Track 8

9

Exercises 7–8.

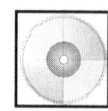

Tonic Chord Patterns

Exercise 7

TRACK 9: Listen to each pattern. In the following measure, make up a different tonic pattern. This made-up pattern may be any combination of Do–Mi–Sol different from the one sung to you. The first time, improvise your patterns on a neutral syllable, and improvise using solfege syllables the second time.

Exercise 8

A. TRACK 10: Follow the score for **Exercise 8** to track the sound. Listen to each pattern sung individually. In the following measure, audiate the pattern you just heard. (Hear it without singing it.) All the patterns will be sung first on a neutral syllable and then on solfege syllables when the exercise is repeated.

B. TRACK 10: Listen to this track again, and in the measure following each pattern sing back the pattern you just heard sung for you.

Tonic Chord Patterns

Track 10

Eb is Do

Dee dee dee
(Do Sol Do)
Dee dee dee
Do Mi Sol
Dee dee dee
Do Mi Sol
Dee dee dee
Sol Mi Do
Dee dee dee
Sol Mi Do

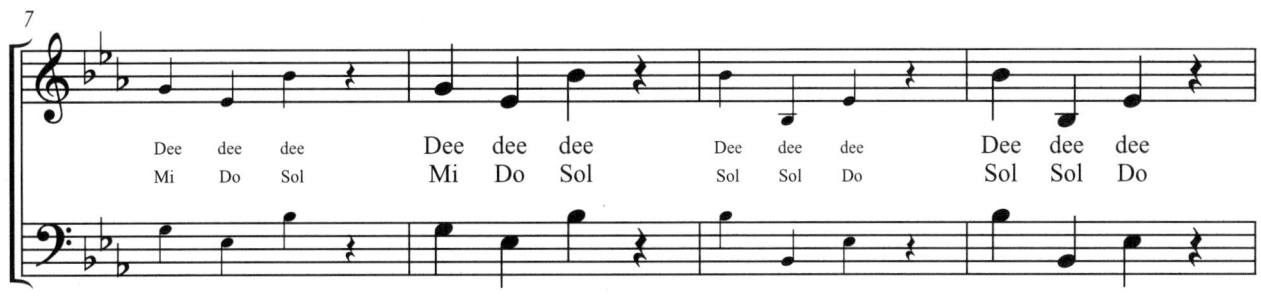

Dee dee dee
Mi Do Sol
Dee dee dee
Mi Do Sol
Dee dee dee
Sol Sol Do
Dee dee dee
Sol Sol Do

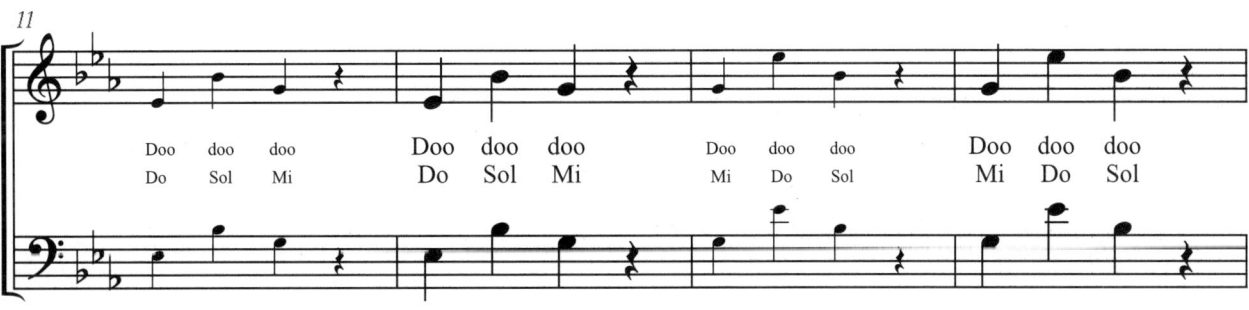

Doo doo doo
Do Sol Mi
Doo doo doo
Do Sol Mi
Doo doo doo
Mi Do Sol
Doo doo doo
Mi Do Sol

Doo doo doo
Sol Mi Sol
Doo doo doo
Sol Mi Sol
Doo doo doo
Do Sol Do
Doo doo doo
Do Sol Do

Tonic Chord Patterns

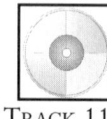

| Exercise 9 | |   |

TRACK 11: Each pattern is repeated four times. In this exercise, *you sing the pattern first* on "dee" or "doo" and the vocal model echoes you. Then, you sing the pattern on solfege syllables echoed by the vocal model. This will allow you to check your accuracy and make any necessary corrections.

Tonic Chord Patterns

Track 11

E♭ is Do

Dee dee dee   Dee dee dee   Mi Do Sol   Mi Do Sol   Dee dee dee

Dee dee dee   Sol Sol Do   Sol Sol Do   Doo doo doo   Doo doo doo

Do Sol Mi   Do Sol Mi   Doo doo doo   Doo doo doo   Mi Do Sol

Mi Do Sol   Doo doo doo   Doo doo doo   Sol Mi Sol   Sol Mi Sol

Doo doo doo   Doo doo doo   Do Sol Do   Do Sol Do

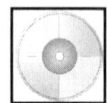

Tonic Chord Patterns

Exercise 10

TRACK 10: Without looking at the score, listen to each pattern. In the following measure, make up a different tonic pattern. This made-up pattern may be any combination of Do–Mi–Sol different from the one sung to you. The first time, improvise your patterns on a neutral syllable, and improvise using solfege syllables the second time.

Exercise 11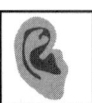

TRACK 12: After a two-measure introduction for each key, improvise eight tonic patterns in each key and sing them on neutral syllables.

UNIT II

DOMINANT CHORD INVERSIONS
AND PATTERNS

Tonic Chord Solfege Syllable Pronunciation Guide

Actual Written Syllable	Correct Pronunciation
Sol	**Soo** The tongue must lie flat in the mouth with the tip of the tongue resting lightly behind the font teeth. Imagine there is a pit in the tongue. The lips should look like "oo" and be rounded but without tension.
Ti	**Tee** Tongue position is high with the tip of the tongue anchored against the lower front teeth. The lips should be slightly rounded to promote focus in the vowel.
Re	**Ree** This should be pronounced exactly as the "tee" above, but beginning with a flipped "r." If experiencing difficulty with the flipped "r," sing a soft "d" in its place.
Fa	**Fah** This vowel is very problematic for amateur choral singers. The American "ah" is generally not high and forward enough. This vowel should be sung as a bright Italian "ah."

Dominant Seventh Chord Inversions

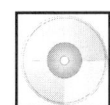

Tracks 13–17

Exercise 12

LISTEN ONLY

    A. Track 13: Listen to the different inversions of the dominant seventh chord.

    B. After you have absorbed the patterns, audiate them. (Hear them inside your head, without the sound being present.)

    C. Track 14: Audiate the inversions while listening to the accompaniment track.

Exercise 13

LISTEN AND SING

    A. Track 15: The inversions will be sung one at a time on neutral syllables. Echo the pattern in the space following each inversion.

    B. Track 16: Listen to the inversions sung on solfege syllables.

    C. Track 17: The inversions will be sung one at a time on solfege syllables. Echo the pattern in the space following each inversion.

Exercise 14.

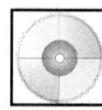

TRACKS 13, 16

Exercise 14

LISTEN, SING, AND FOLLOW THE SCORE

A. TRACK 13: Follow the score for **Exercise 14** as you listen.

B. TRACK 13: Follow the score and sing along with Track 13 on neutral syllables. (Two different keys are used for these exercises so you can become familiar with reading the dominant chord on spaces as well as lines.)

C. TRACK 16: Follow the score and sing along with Track 16 on solfege syllables.

Dominant Seventh Inversions

Tracks 13 and 16

Tracks 13 and 16: When the dominant chord is used in the music, it does not always include Fa, the seventh of the chord. We have included it in these inversions, however, so that you can hear how the dominant seventh chord leads back to the tonic chord.

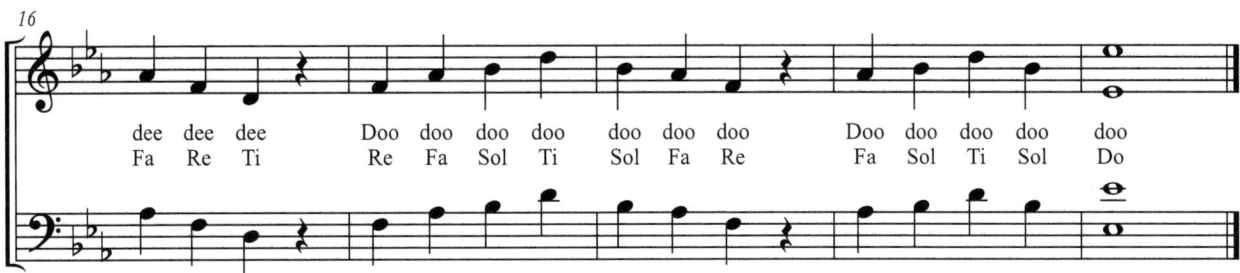

19

Dominant Chord Patterns

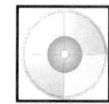

TRACKS 18–19

Exercise 15

LISTEN ONLY

TRACK 18: Listen to the dominant chord patterns along with the aural accompaniment anchors sounding the tonic and dominant. (There is no score for this exercise.)

Exercise 16

LISTEN, SING, AND FOLLOW THE SCORE

A. TRACK 19: Follow the score for **Exercise 16** to track the sound. Listen to each pattern sung individually. In the following measure, audiate the pattern you just heard. (Hear it without singing it.) All the patterns will be sung first on a neutral syllable and then on solfege syllables when the exercise is repeated.

B. TRACK 19: Listen to this track again, and in the measure following each pattern sing the pattern you just heard sung for you.

SCORE NOTES: The first two systems have dominant chords without the seventh of the chord indicated by the Roman numeral V above the measure. In the last two systems, the chord symbol V7 indicates that the pattern includes Fa, the seventh of the chord. Both halves of this exercise end on a tonic chord as indicated by the Roman numeral I.

Dominant Chord Patterns

Track 19

Dominant Chord Patterns

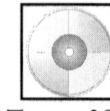

TRACK 20

Exercise 17

READ THE SCORE, SING, AND LISTEN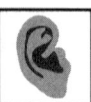

Track 20: Each pattern is repeated four times. In this exercise, *you sing the pattern first* on "dee" or "doo," and the vocal model echoes you. Then, you sing the pattern on solfege syllables, echoed again by the vocal model. This will allow you to check your accuracy and make any necessary corrections.

Dominant Chord Patterns

Track 20

22

Exercise 18–19.

Dominant Chord Patterns

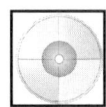

TRACKS 19, 21

Exercise 18

LISTEN AND SING

TRACK 19: Without looking at the score, listen to each pattern. In the following measure, make up a different dominant pattern. This made-up pattern may be any combination of Sol–Ti–Re–(Fa) different from the one sung to you. The first time, improvise your patterns on a neutral syllable, and improvise using solfege syllables the second time.

Exercise 19

LISTEN, SING, AND FOLLOW THE SCORE

A. TRACK 21: Follow the score for **Exercise 19** to track the sound. Listen to each pattern sung individually. In the following measure, audiate the pattern you just heard. (Hear it without singing it.) All the patterns will be sung first on a neutral syllable and then on solfege syllables when the exercise is repeated.

B. TRACK 21: Listen to this track again, and in the measure following each pattern sing back the pattern you just heard sung for you.

Dominant Chord Patterns

Track 21

Track 21: In this exercise, the dominant seventh chords are interspersed throughout.

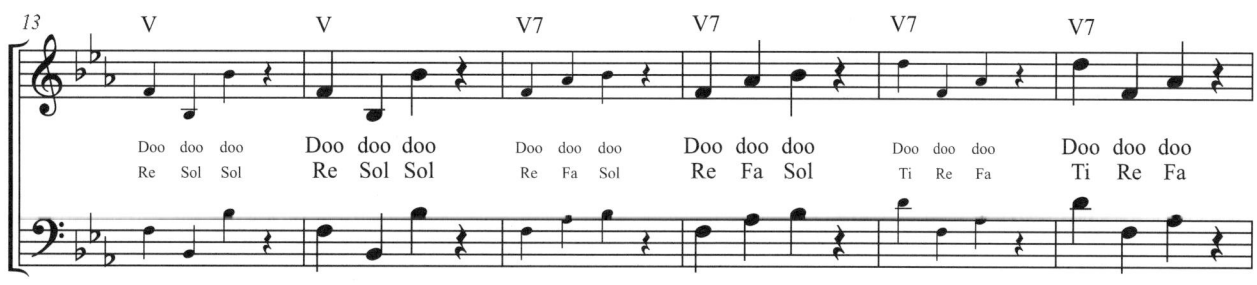

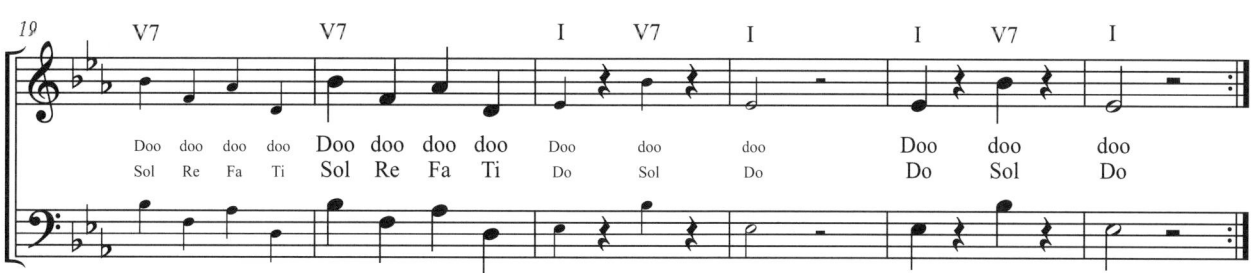

Exercise 20.

Dominant Chord Patterns

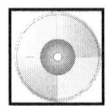

TRACK 22

Exercise 20

READ THE SCORE, SING, AND LISTEN	  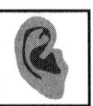

TRACK 22: Each pattern is repeated four times. In this exercise, *you sing the pattern first*, and the vocal model echoes after you. Then, you sing the pattern again on solfege syllables, echoed again by the vocal model. This will allow you to check your accuracy and make any necessary corrections.

Dominant Chord Patterns

Track 22

Exercise 20.

Dominant Chord Patterns

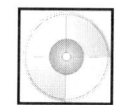

TRACKS 21, 23

Exercise 21

LISTEN AND SING

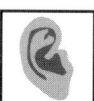 

TRACK 21: Without looking at the score, listen to each pattern. In the following measures, make up a different dominant pattern. This made-up pattern may be any combination of Sol–Ti–Re–(Fa) different from the one sung to you. The first time, improvise your patterns on a neutral syllable, and improvise using solfege syllables the second time.

Exercise 22

LISTEN AND SING

TRACK 23: After a two-measure introduction, improvise four dominant or dominant seventh patterns, singing them on neutral syllable. The accompaniment resolves to tonic, after which you improvise four new patterns. The modulation occurs, and you have the opportunity to improvise four new patterns, followed by tonic and more improvisation.

UNIT III

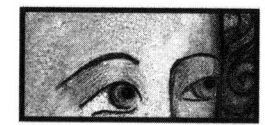

SUBDOMINANT CHORD
INVERSIONS AND PATTERNS

Subdominant Chord Solfege Syllable Pronunciation Guide

Actual Written Syllable	Correct Pronunciation
Fa	**Fah** As pronounced in the dominant chord solfege with vowel high and forward as in a bright Italian "ah."
La	**Lah** This syllable has the same vowel problem as "Fa." The "ah" vowel should be sung similarly to the bright Italian "ah." An additional problem is the American pronunciation of "l." The "l" must be executed with the tip of the tongue, as the normal American "l" will cause the placement of the vowel to be incorrect.
Do	**Doo** As pronounced in the tonic chord solfege with an imaginary pit in the tongue and the tip of the tongue resting lightly behind the front teeth. The lips should look like "oo" and be rounded but without tension.

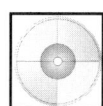

Tonic, Dominant, and Subdominant Inversions —Arpeggiated Cadences

TRACKS 24–28

Exercise 23

LISTEN ONLY

A. TRACK 24: Subdominant inversions must be heard in context with the tonic and dominant chords you've learned so far. Therefore, you will hear a progression of chords: tonic–subdominant–tonic–dominant seventh–tonic (I–IV–I–V7–I). This progression is referred to as a cadence. You will hear the cadence arpeggiated in root position and two inversions. Listen to Track 24 until these sounds are imbedded in your subconscious! These three chords form the keystone of all progressions that follow.

B. After you have absorbed the arpeggiated cadence and its inversions, audiate each (hear each of them inside your head without the sound being present).

C. TRACK 25: Audiate the arpeggiated cadence while listening to the accompaniment track.

Exercise 24

LISTEN AND SING

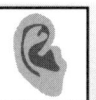 

A. TRACK 26: Each arpeggiated chord of the cadence will be sung one at a time on neutral syllables. Echo in the accompaniment measures following each chord.

B. TRACK 27: Listen to the arpeggiated cadence sung on solfege syllables.

C. TRACK 28: Each arpeggiated chord of the cadence will be sung one at a time on solfege syllables. Echo in the accompaniment measures following each chord.

Exercise 25.

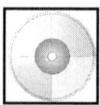

TRACKS 24, 27

Exercise 25

LISTEN, SING, AND FOLLOW THE SCORE

A. TRACK 24: Follow the score for **Exercise 25** as you listen.

B. TRACK 24: Follow the score and sing along on neutral syllables. (Two different keys are used for these exercises so you can become familiar with reading the subdominant chord on lines as well as spaces.)

C. TRACK 27: Follow the score and sing along with Track 27 on solfege syllables.

Tonic, Dominant, and Subdominant Inversions

Arpeggiated Cadences

Track 24 and 27

Exercises 26–27.

Subdominant Chord Patterns

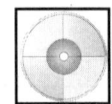

TRACKS 29–30

Exercise 26

LISTEN ONLY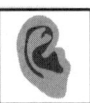

TRACK 29: Listen to the subdominant chord patterns that begin and end with an accompaniment cadence resolving to tonic. (There is no score for this exercise.)

Exercise 27

LISTEN, SING, AND FOLLOW THE SCORE

A. TRACK 30: Follow the score for **Exercise 27** to track the sound. Listen to each pattern sung individually. In the following measure, audiate the pattern you just heard (hear it without singing it). All the patterns will be sung first on a neutral syllable and then on solfege syllables when the exercise is repeated.

B. TRACK 30: Listen to this track again, and in the measure following each pattern sing back the pattern you just heard sung for you.

Subdominant Chord Patterns

Track 30

Exercise 28.

Subdominant Chord Patterns

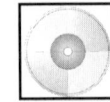

Exercise 28

READ THE SCORE, SING, AND LISTEN

Track 31: Each pattern is repeated four times. In this exercise, *you sing the pattern first*, and the vocal model echoes after you. Then, you sing the pattern on solfege syllables, echoed again by the vocal model. This will allow you to check your accuracy and make any necessary corrections.

Subdominant Chord Patterns

Track 31

40

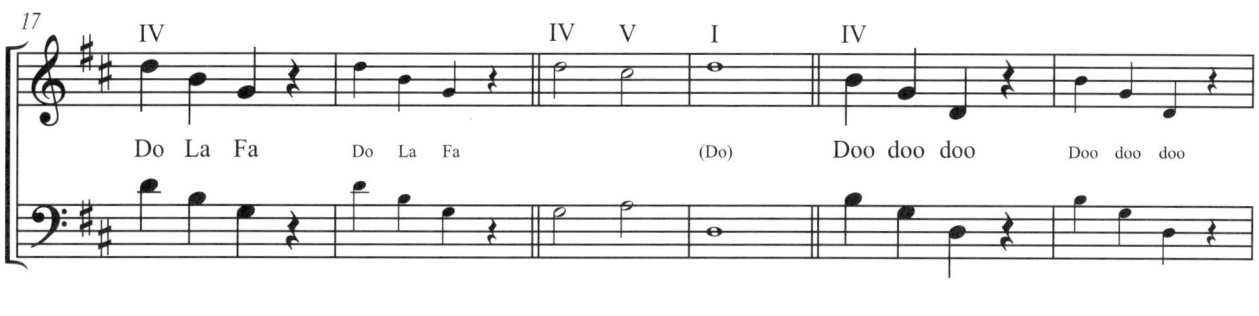

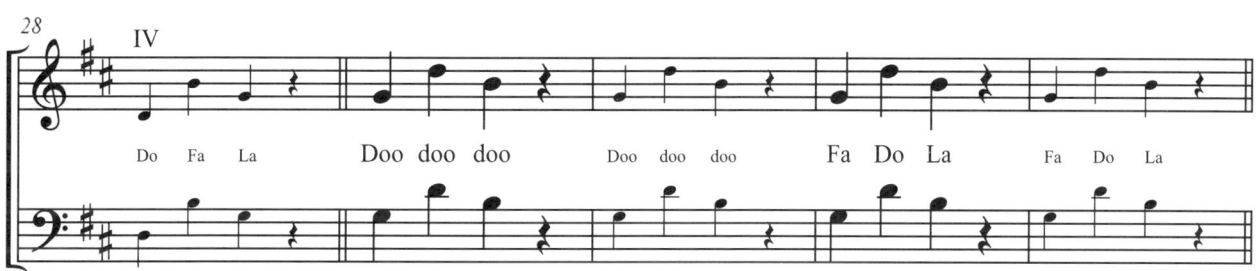

41

Subdominant Chord Patterns

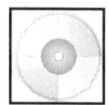

TRACKS 30, 32

Exercise 29

LISTEN AND SING

TRACK 30: Without looking at the score, listen to each pattern. In the following measure, make up a different subdominant pattern. This made-up pattern may be any combination of Fa–La–Do different from the one sung to you. The first time, improvise your patterns on a neutral syllable, and improvise using solfege syllables the second time.

Exercise 30

LISTEN, SING, AND FOLOW SCORE

A. TRACK 32: Follow the score for **Exercise 30** to track the sound. Listen to each pattern sung individually. In the following measure, audiate the pattern you just heard (hear it without singing it). All the patterns will be sung first on a neutral syllable and then on solfege syllables when the exercise is repeated.

B. TRACK 32: Listen to this track again, and in the measure following each pattern sing back the pattern you just heard sung for you.

Subdominant Chord Patterns

Track 32

Subdominant Chord Patterns

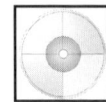

Exercise 31

READ THE SCORE, SING, AND LISTEN

TRACK 33: Each pattern is repeated four times. In this exercise, *you sing the pattern first*, and the vocal model echoes you. Then, you sing the pattern on solfege syllables, echoed again by the vocal model. This will allow you to check your accuracy and make any necessary corrections.

Subdominant Chord Patterns

Track 33

Subdominant Chord Patterns

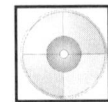

Exercise 32

LISTEN AND SING

TRACK 32: Without looking at the score, listen to each pattern. In the following measure, make up a different subdominant pattern. This made-up pattern may be any combination of Fa–La–Do different from the one sung to you. The first time, improvise your patterns on a neutral syllable, and improvise using solfege syllables the second time.

Exercise 33

LISTEN AND SING

TRACK 34: After a two-measure introductory cadence, improvise four subdominant patterns. You will then hear a two-measure cadence after which you may improvise another four patterns. Repeat this sequence in the new key after the modulation.

UNIT IV

CHORD PROGRESSIONS WITH TONIC, DOMINANT, SUBDOMINANT

Subdominant Chord Solfege Syllable Pronunciation Guide

Actual Written Syllable	Correct Pronunciation
Do	**Doo** Imagine there is a pit in the tongue. The lips should look like "oo" and be rounded
Re	**Ree** Tongue position is high with the tip of the tongue anchored against the lower front teeth. Wrap lips around the vowel.
Mi	**Mee** Tongue position is high with the tip of the tongue anchored against the lower front teeth. Wrap lips around the vowel.
Fa	**Fah** This vowel should be sung as a bright Italian "ah," very forward and high.
Sol	**Soo** Imagine there is a pit in the tongue. The lips should look like "oo" and be rounded.
La	**Lah** This vowel should be sung as a bright Italian "ah," very forward and high. Use a tip-of-the-tongue "l."
Ti	**Tee** Tongue position is high with the tip of the tongue anchored against the lower front teeth. Wrap lips around the vowel.

Four-Measure Progressions

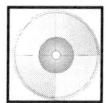

Exercise 34

LISTEN ONLY

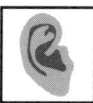

A. TRACK 35: Listen to the eight four-measure chord progressions. Each is based on the tonic, subdominant, and dominant chord patterns you learned in Units I, II, and III.

B. TRACK 37: Listen to the progressions sung on solfege syllables.

Four-Measure Progressions

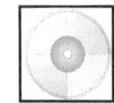

Exercise 35

LISTEN, SING, AND FOLLOW THE SCORE

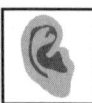

A.   TRACK 36: Follow the score for Exercises 35–36 to track the sound. The progression will be sung one at a time on neutral syllables. Audiate the progression in the following accompaniment measures. Two different keys are used for these progressions so you can have the opportunity to read all the patterns you have practiced.

B.   TRACK 36: Listen to this track again. After the vocal model sings the progression, sing it back on neutral syllables in the accompaniment measures following each progression.

Exercise 36

LISTEN, SING, AND FOLLOW THE SCORE

TRACK 38: Follow the score for Exercises 35–36. The progressions will be sung one at a time on solfege syllables. After the vocal model sings the progression, sing it back on solfege syllables in the accompaniment measures following each progression.

Chord Progressions

Tracks 36, 38

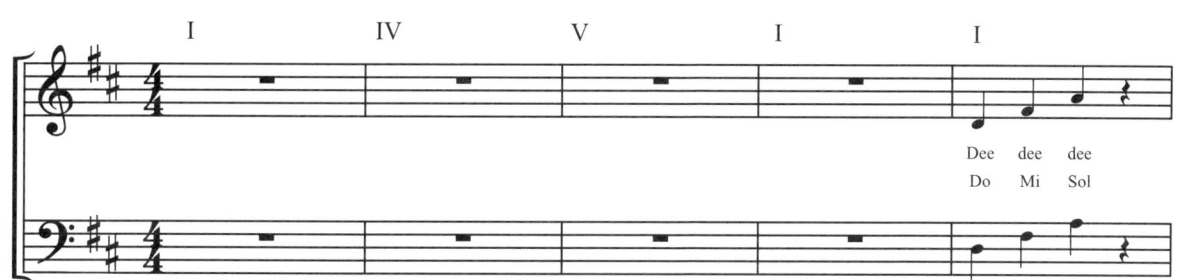

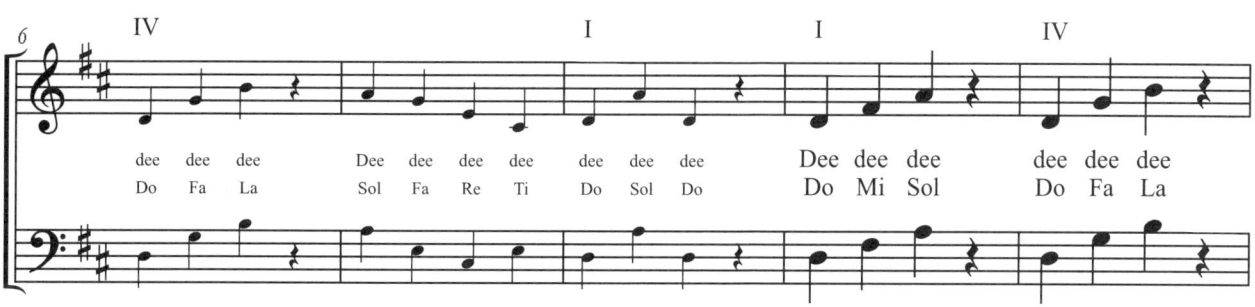

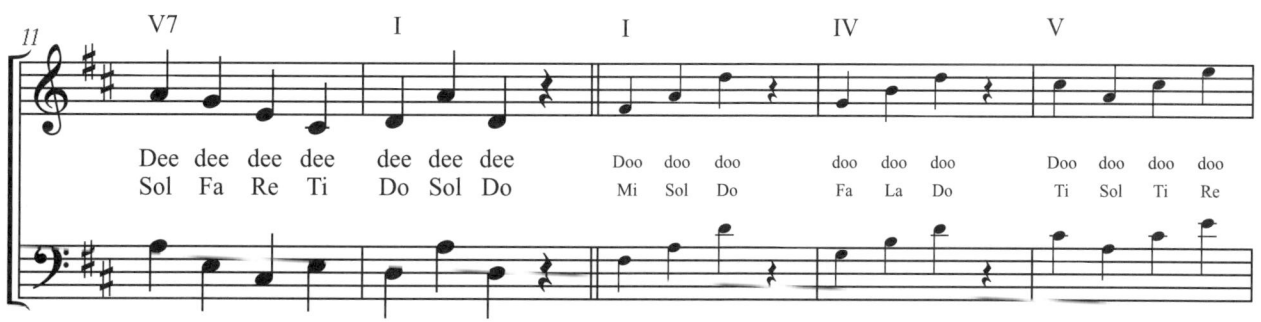

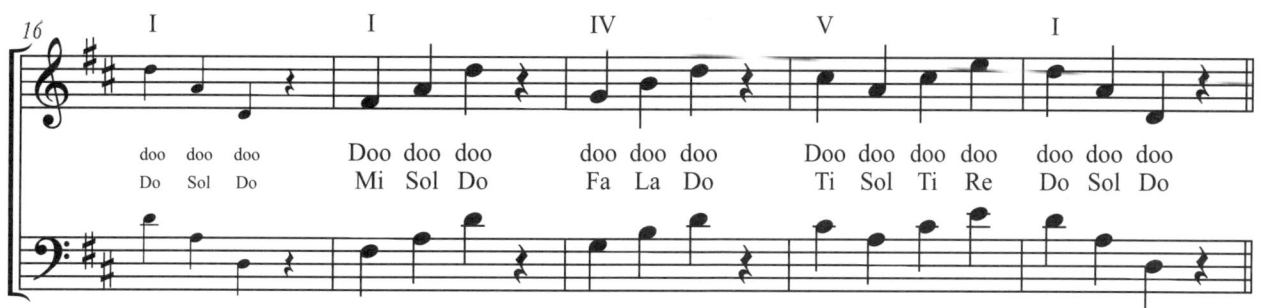

Exercises 35–36.

Chord Progression Round

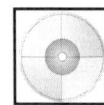

Exercise 37

LISTEN AND SING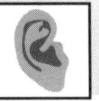

A. TRACK 39: As you listen to the accompanied round, see if you can identify the chords.

B. TRACK 40: Sing the root of each chord as you listen to the round sung this time with a bass part played on string bass. Sing the roots first on a neutral syllable and then on solfege.

Exercise 38

LISTEN, SING, AND FOLLOW THE SCORE

A. TRACK 39: As you follow the music for **Exercise 38**, listen again.

B. TRACK 39: Sing the round in unison with the vocal model.

C. TRACK 41: Two-part round – The vocal model will begin first. When she has completed the first system, you start at the beginning. You will be singing a two-part round with the voice on the recording.

D. TRACK 42: Three-part round – The vocal models will begin first. When the second singer completes the first system, you start at the beginning. You will be singing a three-part round with the voices on the recording.

E. TRACK 43: Four-part round – Repeat what you did for the three-part round. A fourth voice will enter after you.

F. TRACK 44: Keyboard accompaniment with aural anchors for use with classroom applications.

Chord Progression Round

Tracks 39–44

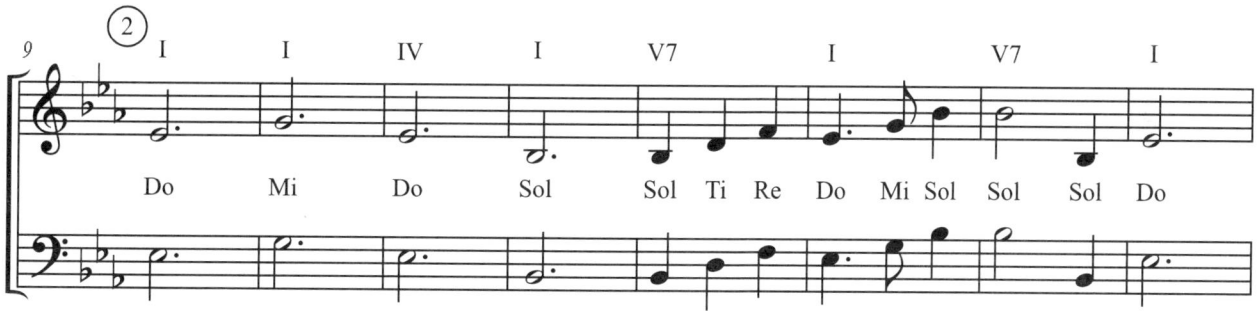

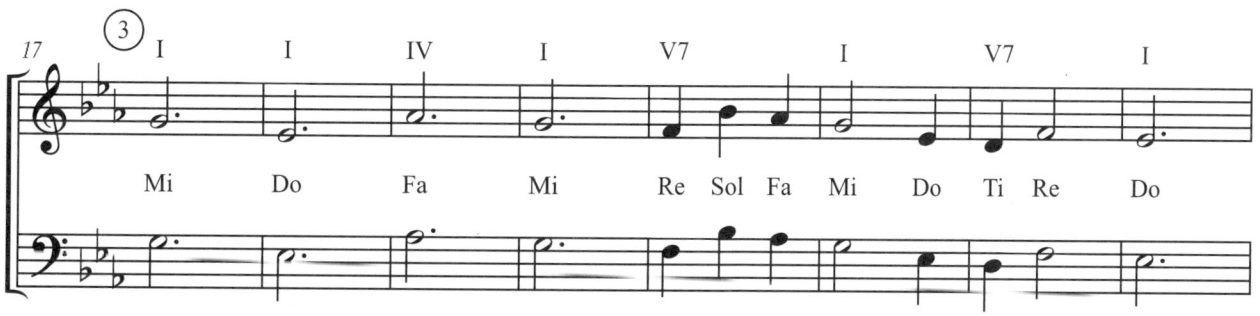